WOODLAND PUBLIC LIBRARY

D0436253

J
629.45
COL
1995

# COUNTDOWN TO SPACE

# APOLLO 13
## Space Emergency

## Michael D. Cole

Series Advisor:
John E. McLeaish
Chief, Public Information Office, retired,
NASA Johnson Space Center

ENSLOW PUBLISHERS, INC.

| 44 Fadem Road | P.O. Box 38 |
| Box 699 | Aldershot |
| Springfield, N.J. 07081 | Hants GU12 6BP |
| U.S.A. | U.K. |

WOODLAND PUBLIC LIBRARY

Copyright © 1995 by Michael D. Cole.

All rights reserved.

No part of this book may be reproduced by any means
without the written permission of the publisher.

**Library of Congress Cataloging-in-Publication Data**

Cole, Michael D.
    Apollo 13: space emergency / Michael D. Cole.
       p. cm. — (Countdown to space)
    Includes bibliographical references and index.
    ISBN 0-89490-542-2
    1. Apollo 13 (Spacecraft)—Juvenile literature. 2. Project Apollo (U.S.)—Juvenile
literature. 3. Space vehicle accidents—Juvenile literature. [1. Apollo 13 (Spacecraft)
2. Project Apollo (U.S.) 3. Space vehicle accidents.] I. Title. II. Series: Cole, Michael D.
Countdown to space.
TL789.8.U6A5267   1995
629.45'4— dc20
                                                    94-41179
                                                      CIP
                                                      AC

Printed in the U.S.A.

10 9 8 7 6 5 4 3 2

**Illustration Credits:**
National Aeronautics and Space Administration (NASA), pp. 4, 6, 7, 8, 9,
10, 12, 15, 17, 19, 21, 22, 26, 28, 32, 35, 36, 39, 40, 41.

**Cover Illustration:**
National Aeronautics and Space Administration (NASA) (foreground);
© L. Manning/Westlight (background).

# CONTENTS

*Happiness showed on the faces of* Apollo 13 *astronauts (from left) Fred Haise, James Lovell, and John Swigert as they emerged from the rescue helicopter.*

# "Houston, We've Had a Problem"

Many people believe that the number thirteen is an unlucky number. But the U.S. space program did not depend on luck.

American astronauts had already landed on the Moon with *Apollo 11* and *Apollo 12*. Those missions had been successful because of hard work and long months of training, not luck.

So NASA (National Aeronautics and Space Administration) ignored superstition. They went ahead and named the next mission *Apollo 13.*

The mission began on April 11, 1970. *Apollo 13* lifted off at 2:13 P.M. from the launchpad at Cape Kennedy in Florida. It was an hour earlier at Mission Control in Houston, Texas. The controllers in Houston watched

*Apollo 13* leave the pad at 1:13 P.M. Houston time. On the military time clock it was 13:13 hours.

"Good luck. Head for the hills," said a controller to the crew of James A. Lovell, Jr., John L. Swigert, Jr., and Fred W. Haise, Jr.[1] The controller was talking about the crew's planned destination on the Moon. Lovell and Haise were supposed to land on the Moon in an area called the Fra Mauro uplands.

Fra Mauro was the site of a huge meteor crater near the Moon's equator. Scientists hoped the original impact of the meteor millions of years ago had blasted samples of the Moon's inner bedrock up to the surface. *Apollo 13*'s astronauts were going to collect samples of this

Apollo 13 *blasted off from Cape Kennedy in Florida on the afternoon of April 11, 1970.*

bedrock so that scientists could learn more about the structure of the Moon.

Strange things started to happen just minutes after they launched the flight. One of the second-stage engines shut down more than two minutes early. The men in Houston corrected the problem. They fired the other four engines thirty-four seconds longer to make up for the lost thrust. Then the third-stage engine fired for nine extra seconds. *Apollo 13* entered Earth orbit in good shape, but they were forty-four seconds behind schedule.

The problems were corrected before the third-stage engine fired again. This "burn" sent *Apollo 13* out of

*The crew of* Apollo 13 *consisted of astronauts (from left to right) Fred W. Haise, Jr., John L. Swigert, Jr., and James A. Lovell, Jr.*

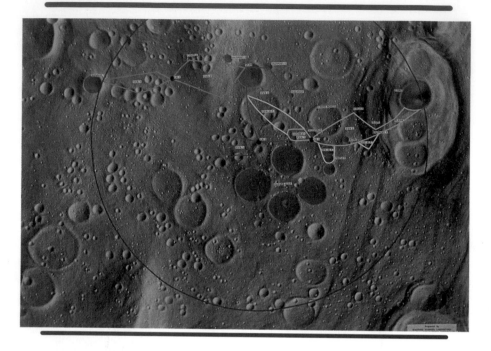

*This hilly region of the Moon known as the Fra Mauro uplands was
Apollo 13's intended landing site.*

Earth orbit and put it on course to arrive at the Moon
in three days.

Hours later Jack Swigert—the command module
pilot—separated the command and service module
(CSM) from the third-stage rocket. The command
module was named *Odyssey* on this flight. Swigert
turned the ship until it was facing back at the rocket.
Next he moved in and docked with the lunar module
(LM). This module was housed inside the rocket
assembly. The lunar module was named *Aquarius*.

Swigert then flipped a switch and *Aquarius* was

separated from the rocket. *Odyssey* and *Aquarius,* now docked head to head, then continued toward the Moon.

For the next two days the flight was very routine. The flight was so routine that the media paid little attention to the mission. The TV networks no longer carried the live broadcasts that the astronauts made from space. Instead the broadcasts were taped, and small parts of them were shown later during the regular network news programs.

The three men had just finished one of their broadcasts when the mission suddenly turned frightening.

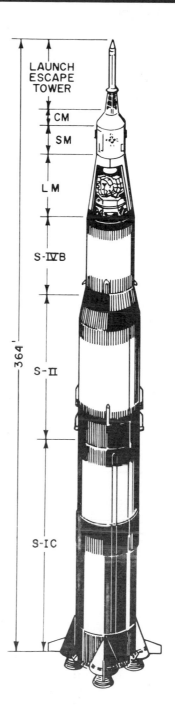

*The diagram of* Apollo 13 *shows the location of the command module (CM), service module (SM), and lunar module (LM) inside the rocket assembly.*

The date was April 13.

The crew was getting ready for an evening period of rest. Suddenly they heard a loud bang. A strong vibration shook the spacecraft.

Lovell was floating above his seat in the command module. He turned to look at Haise, who was floating in the tunnel that led to the lunar module hatch. Lovell thought Haise had made the sound by opening a valve in the lunar module. But Lovell saw the look of concern on Haise's face when the spacecraft shook. Haise had not opened any valve. The bang had been something else.[2]

Swigert was in his couch in the command module. A master alarm was sounding in his headset. A yellow warning light on the instrument panel in front of him

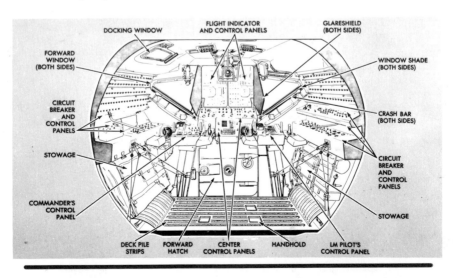

This diagram of the crew compartment of Apollo 13 shows the control panels of the spacecraft.

signalled a major loss of electrical power in the spacecraft. He slid across to the right couch and looked at the electrical system readouts. The voltage was dropping.

"Okay Houston, we've had a problem here," Swigert said. His words took the controllers in Houston by surprise.

"This is Houston, say again please."

"Houston, we've had a problem," Lovell said. He too was looking at the electrical readouts. "We've had a main B bus undervolt." This meant that the electrical power produced by one of the ship's three fuel cells was dropping. In fact, the fuel cell soon had no power at all.

"Roger. Main B undervolt," Houston said. "Okay, stand by *13*. We're looking at it."[3]

More warning lights lit up on the display panel in the next three minutes. It soon appeared that fuel cells 1 and 3 were both dead. This situation automatically cancelled the Moon landing mission. They could not make the trip on only one operating fuel cell. The astronauts were very disappointed.[4]

Lovell continued to check all the systems aboard the spacecraft. The outlook grew worse. He was stunned when he noticed the quantity indicator light on oxygen tank 2. It read zero.[5] Their situation was serious.

They were losing oxygen.

The oxygen was needed for several purposes aboard

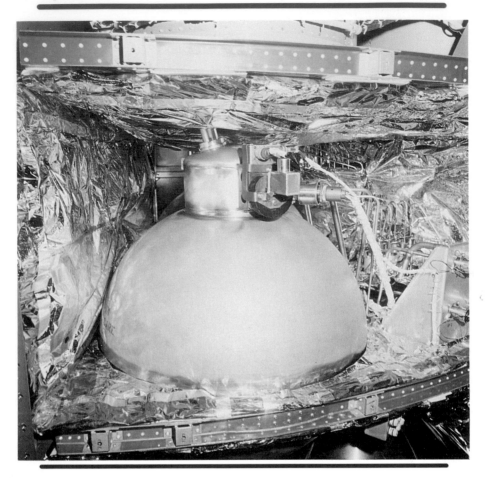

*This photo, taken prior to launch, shows the* Apollo 13 *service module. The oxygen tank shown is the one that astronaut Jim Lovell noticed read "zero."*

the spacecraft. But most important, the astronauts needed it to *breathe.*

The oxygen in the tanks was also used to react with hydrogen in the ship's fuel cells. The energy produced by this chemical reaction within the fuel cells provided all the electrical power in the spacecraft. Without proper quantities of oxygen, the fuel cells would not work. And if they did not work, electrical power in the spacecraft would fail.

There were three oxygen tanks aboard, but the level in oxygen tank 2 was now zero. There were only two oxygen tanks left to make power in the one remaining fuel cell.

A moment later Lovell looked at the quantity indicator light for oxygen tank 1. It too was dropping slowly as he watched it. He couldn't believe it.

Lovell was the mission commander. He was responsible for the lives of his crew. He watched the quantity level on oxygen tank 1 go down. Suddenly he realized that he and his crew might not make it home alive.[6]

## 2

# No Turning Back

James Lovell was trying to figure out what had happened to *Apollo 13*. Two out of three fuel cells had shut down. One oxygen tank was empty. The level in another one was dropping. Only one good oxygen tank remained to operate the only remaining fuel cell.

They might soon be unable to generate any electrical power on the ship.

What had happened?

Lovell floated over to look out his window. He was not surprised to find a cloud of mist. "It looks to me that we are venting something," Lovell said. "We are venting something out into space."[1]

In Houston, chief flight director Gene Kranz tried to keep things under control. "Okay, let's everybody think of the kind of things we'd be venting," he said.

No one could identify anything that would normally be venting. It was most likely the oxygen.

"Okay, now let's everybody keep cool," Kranz said. "We've got LM still attached, let's make sure we don't blow the whole mission."[2]

Kranz was right about the lunar module. Whatever was wrong with the command module, it did not affect the attached lunar module. Kranz ordered the crew to power down the command module. This would conserve its power until they could learn exactly what was wrong. Even as they shut it down, *Odyssey* continued to lose power.

*In Houston at Mission Control, chief flight director Gene Kranz (foreground, back to camera) tried to keep things under control. Astronaut Fred Haise is seen on the screen.*

The astronauts were in a tough spot. But they did not have time to consider what a grim situation they were in. There was lots of work to do, so they simply got to it. Worrying or panicking would not make their situation better. And their situation was definitely not good.

It became clear to the crew and the people in Houston that there had been an explosion aboard *Odyssey.* The explosion had ruptured oxygen tank 2 and was causing a slow leak in tank 1. The explosion had also damaged two of the three fuel cells.

In other words, the command module was crippled. The lunar module would have to become the astronauts' lifeboat.

The lunar module was designed to support two men for two days. Now it would have to support three men for four days. *Apollo 13* was 45,000 miles away from the Moon. They were five times that distance from Earth.

There could be no turning back. They could not generate enough power to make a direct return to Earth. They would have to make the trip around the Moon.

During the swing around the Moon, the LM's landing engine would fire and set *Apollo 13* on a trajectory back toward Earth. The lunar module's engine had never been used for that before.

There was one other problem. The lunar module

*It became clear to Mission Control in Houston that an explosion had taken place aboard* Odyssey. *Here two flight directors discuss critical maneuvers of* Apollo 13 *after the accident.*

had no heatshield. It could not enter Earth's atmosphere. Only the command module with its heatshield was designed to reenter.

Lovell, Swigert, and Haise hung their hopes on two things. The first was that the lunar module could make the engine burn on the other side of the Moon and keep them alive until they could return to Earth. The second was that when they arrived at Earth, the command module would still have enough power to make a safe reentry. But their chances didn't look good.

The next morning the world woke up to the crisis aboard *Apollo 13*. People had not known much about the mission up until then. But by evening, people around the world were well aware of the dangers the astronauts faced.[3]

Newspapers, radio, and television brought news and updates about the crippled mission. Soon millions of people everywhere were familiar with the names of James Lovell, Jack Swigert, and Fred Haise.

Lovell and Haise were now in the lunar module *Aquarius*. Swigert stayed in the command module *Odyssey*. At the same time as Swigert was shutting down the command module, Lovell and Haise powered up *Aquarius*. Swigert used as little power as possible in *Odyssey*. He used only the cabin lights, the radio, and the heaters that would keep the reentry guidance systems ready at the end of the mission. Swigert later joined Lovell and Haise in *Aquarius*.

Engineers and technicians who had worked on the Apollo spacecrafts began to gather in Houston. They worked on new plans to help bring the crew home. A whole new return trajectory plan would have to be calculated and tested.

Other astronauts spent hours in the spacecraft simulators. They tested the engine burns and maneuvers the crew would be using to get home. The plans seemed to work in the simulators. Everyone hoped they would work in space.

*Apollo 13* neared the Moon. Fred Haise took a turn at sleeping in the darkened command module. They had been in space for sixty-nine hours. When Haise awoke, Lovell and Swigert took their turn to sleep. While they slept, some major decisions were being made in Houston.

The engine burn to bring the astronauts home would be made in several hours. There were disagreements on how to do it. Some people at Houston wanted to make a superfast burn that would get the astronauts home almost two days earlier. To do this, the service module part of the command module would have to be discarded. Only the crew capsule of the command module would be left. This would reduce the weight of the two ships by 50 percent.

*Activity at Mission Control became feverish as everyone worked on plans to bring the crew home safely.*

There was a problem with this plan. If they discarded the service module, the capsule's heatshield surface would be exposed to space temperatures for forty hours. No one knew what this would do to the heatshield. It was too risky. No matter when the astronauts returned, a damaged heatshield would mean certain death.

NASA decided to keep the service module attached and make a burn that would bring the crew home in about four days. But would there be enough power to last the entire trip? Would the crew have enough water and oxygen to keep them alive and alert by the time they reentered Earth's atmosphere?

Teams in Houston worked on answering these questions. They worked out schedules for conserving power on the two ships. They worked out a plan for oxygen consumption. Engineers also devised a way that water could be transferred from the backpacks the astronauts would have used on the Moon. The astronauts also tried to build a device that would keep carbon dioxide from building up in the command module.

Many of the problems were being solved. It began to look as if a four-day return trip in the lunar module would work. Power for the ships, and oxygen and water for the crew should last that long. As long as nothing else went wrong.

Lovell got only a short nap in *Odyssey*. The

spacecraft was dark and only minimum lighting was on in the lunar module. *Odyssey* was also becoming cooler. The cold and darkness of the command module gave the three men an eerie feeling.[4] One of their spacecrafts was practically dead. And they were still so far from home.

By now the Moon dominated the view out their windows. It no longer looked like a disk to the three men. They could now see the craters, hills, and mountains of the Moon below them. They got out cameras and took as many pictures as they could. But then there was plenty of work to do.

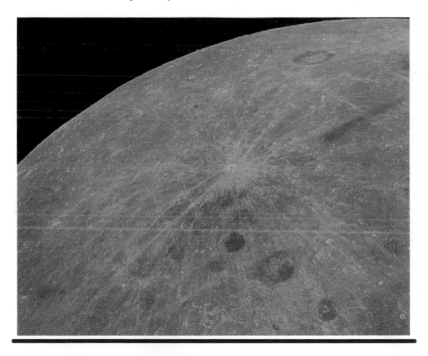

*The* Apollo 13 *crew took this photograph of a bright-rayed crater on the Moon's farside.*

*The* Apollo 13 *crew saw this view of the Moon from their spacecraft.*

All the systems aboard the lunar module had to be charged up for the engine burn. The burn would occur after *Apollo 13* had swung around the Moon and was headed back home.

After seventy-six hours and thirty-two minutes in space, *Apollo 13* went into the shadow of the Moon. About thirty minutes later, the two ships passed behind the Moon and lost contact with Earth. For the next twenty-five minutes the Moon blocked all communications between Houston and *Apollo 13*.

When it emerged once again, the three men were on their way home. Finally the distance between them and Earth was narrowing with each passing second. Now it was time for the engine burn.

Swigert crawled back into *Odyssey*. Haise, who was the lunar module pilot for the mission, stayed in *Aquarius* with Lovell. Lovell threw the switch to start the burn. He and Haise controlled the burn manually for almost five minutes. They felt themselves being pushed toward the floor of the lunar module. Because the engine burn made no sound, this was the only way they could tell the burn was working.

Then the burn was over. Mission Control now showed that *Apollo 13* would arrive at Earth ten hours earlier than it would on a regular return trip. The successful burn was a boost to the astronauts' morale. It looked as if they might make it.[5]

Now there was a new concern to the people at Mission Control. The information they were receiving from the tracking stations was not good.

As *Apollo 13* returned toward Earth, something was pushing it further and further off course. If the drift continued, they would completely miss Earth.

"You guys have really got a tough job right now."

"Well everybody down here is 100 percent optimistic," Lousma assured Haise. "Looks like we're on the top side of the whole thing now."[3]

After three hours, Lovell gave up trying to sleep. He returned to the lunar module and relieved Haise. "This is Lovell here," he said.

Jack Lousma was surprised. "Gee whiz," he said, "you got up kind of early didn't you?"

"It's cold back there in the command module," Lovell explained.[4] The temperature in the command

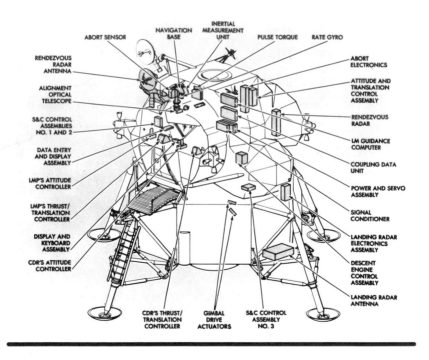

*The diagram of* Apollo 13's *lunar module shows its complex guidance, navigation, and control subsystems. This lunar module acted as the crew's "lifeboat."*

module was about 50°F. And it would get colder. There were two and a half days to go before splashdown.

Lousma suggested they might want to put on their spacesuits to guard against the falling temperatures in the ships. Lovell said no. He thought the bulky suits would make it too difficult to move around.

There were blankets in the emergency landing pack aboard the command module. But they were buried beneath a mound of other equipment. They didn't have the time or energy to dig for them.

The hours rolled by. Swigert joined Lovell in *Aquarius,* so Haise could get some rest. Lovell and Lousma discussed the upcoming course correction. The engine burn would be made in about ten hours.

They still had a long way to go. They could not stop whatever was venting from the spacecraft. And they had not entirely solved the problem of carbon dioxide buildup in the cabin. Lovell and Swigert tried to adapt one of the command module's odor canisters for that purpose.

They used the canister to construct a box. This "mailbox" would filter the carbon dioxide from the air by sucking it through a hose taped to the canister. It was a pretty creative rig, but it looked like it might work.

James Lovell tried to put on a brave face as he worked. He got out a tape and played some music.

Capcom Lousma asked, "You got a Chinese band going up there?"

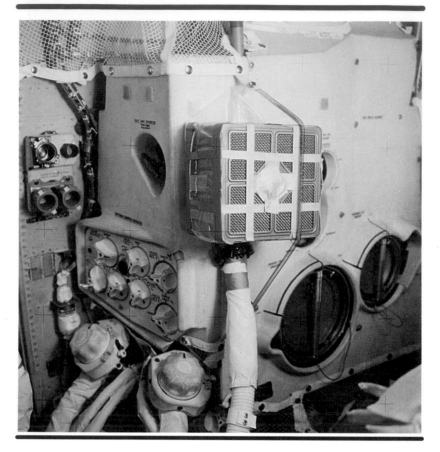

*This interior view of* Apollo 13's *lunar module shows the "mailbox" the astronauts constructed to filter carbon dioxide from the air.*

"Oh, sorry," Lovell said, "I forgot I was on mike."

"Sounds pretty good," Lousma added. The people in Houston were glad to hear the astronauts were keeping their chins up.[5]

It was now April 15. Lovell, Swigert, and Haise had been in space for four days. They would be home in two days—if all went well.

*Apollo 13* was now speeding up as Earth's gravity began to pull on the two ships. This too was a morale booster to the astronauts. But the next forty-eight hours would be the toughest for the crew. The power would remain very low and the cabin temperature would get much colder.

They needed to conserve as much power as possible so they could give a good electrical charge to the reentry battery. This battery would power the command module through reentry. Without a good charge on the battery, Swigert would not be able to control the command module during reentry.

By evening the astronauts were powering up the lunar module for the course correction burn. It took more than an hour to set all the switches in the correct positions for the burn. At 10:30 P.M. Houston time, the lunar module engine fired. It was a difficult procedure.

Swigert watched the time clock. He told Haise when to press the buttons to start and stop the engine. Lovell had his eyes on a telescope. During the burn, he kept the telescope's crosshair on the center of the crescent Earth ahead of him. At the same time he manually fired thrusters to keep it pointed on course. The burn was over in fifteen seconds.

*Apollo 13* was now back on course for a splashdown in the Pacific in about forty hours. The lunar module was powered down again, and the astronauts settled in for some rest. They did not rest well in the growing cold.[6] The temperature in the command module had fallen to about 44°F.

Early on the morning of April 16, Swigert began to switch electrical power from *Aquarius* to the reentry battery in *Odyssey*. It would take fifteen hours to charge the battery. But the power-down procedure in the lunar module had been very successful. It appeared there would be plenty of reserve to charge *Odyssey*'s battery up to full power for reentry.

Now the crew simply needed to last the remaining hours. The command module grew colder and colder. Water droplets were forming on the windows and the instrument panels. Because they had also been conserving their drinking water, Haise had become ill with a kidney infection and could not control his shivering. All three of them had consumed dangerously little water in the last two days. Houston was concerned that the lack of water would affect the astronauts' judgment and reactions during reentry.[7]

The three men were fighting cold, hunger, thirst, and exhaustion. They had overcome some huge problems to get this far toward home. It looked like they might make it, if they could just hang on a little longer.

# 4

# Hanging On

The last twenty-four hours were extremely tough on Lovell, Swigert, and Haise. The explosion had damaged the command module water tank. They had to ration their drinking water. The three men could drink only six ounces of water a day. That was less than one-fifth the normal requirement to keep them in good health. The doctors in Houston hoped the astronauts could still function as dehydration set in.

As the temperature kept falling in the command module, water droplets continued to collect on the walls, windows, and control panels. They worried that the water might collect behind some of the instruments and cause a short-circuit in the controls. Or worse.

If the temperature continued to fall, the controls

could freeze up. It was only about 38°F in the command module. Just a few degrees above freezing.

The cold made the crew's life difficult. Lovell described how his crewmates were sleeping. "It's sort of humorous," he said. "Fred's sleeping place now is in the tunnel, upside down, with his head resting on the ascent engine cover. Jack is on the floor of the lunar module with a restraint harness wrapped around his arm to keep him down there."[1]

Neither man tried to sleep in the command module because of the cold. The capcom for the next shift, Vance Brand, asked Haise about the cold.

*Mission Control remained a close link to the astronauts. During one shift, Capcom Vance Brand (foreground, left) asked Fred Haise about the cold.*

"It's kind of a cold winter day up there isn't it?" he said. "Is it snowing in the command module yet?"

"No, not quite," Haise replied. "The windows are in pretty bad shape . . . every window in the command module is covered with water droplets. It's going to take a lot of scrubbing to get that cleared off."[2]

By evening in Houston, the instrument checklist for reentry was almost ready. They told Swigert he would need plenty of paper to write it down. But there were delays in getting the checklist relayed to the crew. Lovell sharply reminded Mission Control that there was no time for such delays.

"We just can't wait around here to read the procedures all the time up to the burn!" he said. "We've got to get them up here, look at them, and then we've got to sleep!"[3]

Finally it was ready. It took two hours to go through the checklist.

Now everything was done. The astronauts could only wait as *Apollo 13* drew closer to Earth. The command module was getting colder by the minute. Lousma again talked to the crew.

"Wish we could figure out a way to get a hot cup of coffee up to you," Lousma said. "It would taste pretty good right now, wouldn't it?"

"Yes, it sure would," Lovell said. "You don't realize how cold this thing becomes . . . the sun is simply turning on the engine of the service module. It's not getting down to the spacecraft at all." Lovell meant that the command module was facing away from the sun, so that sunlight was falling only on the service module engine directly behind them. The rest of *Apollo 13* was in shadow. If the sun had been shining along the length of the two ships, both spacecrafts would have been much warmer.

"Hang in there. It won't be long," Lousma said.[4]

It was now 3:00 A.M. on the morning of April 17. *Apollo 13* was set to splashdown at about noon. Houston now decided there was enough power left to bring the lunar module up to full power. Two hours later the temperature in *Aquarius* had risen enough to take the chill off the crew.

Swigert later floated into the command module. It had also grown a little warmer in there. "Hey, it's warmed up here now. It's almost comfortable. . . . I'm looking out the window now and that Earth is whistling in like a high-speed freight train."[5]

The command module was finally powered up. To Swigert's relief, the controls and thrusters seemed to be working perfectly. It looked like there would be plenty of power to make the reentry.

The crew now got into position to jettison the damaged service module. The module's failure had almost cost them their lives. Now it separated and drifted slowly away. All three astronauts moved toward windows to get pictures of it. They could not believe what they saw. Lovell spoke first.

*The damaged service module of* Apollo 13, *after it was jettisoned.*

"And there's one whole side of that spacecraft missing!" he said.

"Is that right!" said the communicator in Houston.

"Right by the high-gain antenna, the whole panel is blown out, almost from the base to the engine."[6] The side of the service module was a mess. The explosion had been a big one. As the astronauts looked at the wrecked service module, it was hard to believe they had been able to limp back from the Moon.

*Apollo 13* was now only about 20,000 miles from Earth. They were almost home. The three men moved into the command module, which was now fully powered up. They closed the hatches between the two ships for the last time. With the flip of a switch they set *Aquarius* free. The lunar module had served them well. It had helped save their lives.

"Farewell, *Aquarius.* And we thank you," Mission Control said.

"She was a good ship," Lovell added.[7]

The crew was now on a proper trajectory for reentry. Everyone hoped that the battery and the ship were ready to function. Whether they survived or not, the three astronauts knew their friends in Houston had done everything possible to get them home. As reentry began, Swigert thanked them.

"I know that all of us here want to thank all you guys down there for the very fine job you did," Swigert said. Capsule communicator Joe Kerwin talked Swigert

*The crew of* Apollo 13 *splashes down safely in the Pacific Ocean upon their return to Earth.*

smoothly through the reentry maneuvers. Swigert appreciated Kerwin's calm voice. "You have a good bedside manner, Joe."

"That's the nicest thing anybody has ever said," Kerwin replied.[8]

*Odyssey* then slid into the Earth's atmosphere. The heat caused by reentry friction cut off communications between Houston and the spacecraft. People watching on television or listening on radio around the world waited for the astronauts' voices to emerge from the blackout.

Three minutes passed. The people at Mission Control started to worry. Swigert should have answered by now. Joe Kerwin asked *Apollo 13* to acknowledge again and again. Another thirty seconds passed.

"OK, Joe," came Swigert's voice finally. Soon the parachutes deployed. Cameras on the recovery ship U.S.S. *Iwo Jima* got television pictures of the capsule and its three parachutes. People around the world watched happily as the capsule floated safely toward its splashdown in the Pacific.[9]

*Apollo 13* was home!

# 5

# Lucky Thirteen

Cheers erupted in the Mission Control room. Many of the ground crew wept as they watched the emotional scene on their large monitor.

James Lovell, Jack Swigert, and Fred Haise had survived an incredible ordeal. But their weary smiles were ear to ear when they emerged from the rescue helicopter and waved to the cheering sailors on the recovery ship.[1]

The three men were almost America's first astronauts to die in space. NASA and its people had learned many lessons in trying to get them home. Most important, they found a design flaw in the Apollo command module. This flaw had almost cost the men their lives. (NASA later redesigned the module for the next space flights.)

NASA administrator Thomas Paine said of the flight: "There has never been a happier moment in the United States space program. Although the *Apollo 13* mission must be recorded as a failure, there has never been a more prideful moment."[2]

President Richard Nixon presented the three astronauts with the Presidential Medal of Freedom. It is America's highest civilian award. The same day the astronauts returned, Nixon flew to Houston to present the ground crew with the same award.

Nixon presented the award to both the ground crew

*Cheers erupted at Mission Control as NASA officials learned of* Apollo 13's *successful splashdown.*

*The astronauts of* Apollo 13 *chat with President Richard Nixon soon after splashdown.*

and the astronauts because the mission had been a team effort. Never had NASA and the astronauts worked so hard and so well together. Their hard work and dedication resulted in the happy ending to a life-threatening crisis.

Many people still think the number 13 is bad luck. But *Apollo 13* had not been unlucky. Three men stranded in space halfway to the Moon had come home alive.

*The astronauts of Apollo 13 were honored as heroes upon their safe return. Here John Swigert and James Lovell ride in a Chicago ticker-tape parade.*

# CHAPTER NOTES

## Chapter 1

1. David Baker, *The History of Manned Space Flight* (New York: Crown Publishers, 1982), p. 375.

2. Harry Hurt III, *For All Mankind* (New York: Atlantic Monthly Press, 1988), p. 206.

3. Richard S. Lewis, *The Voyages of Apollo* (New York: The New York Times Book Company, 1974), pp. 158–159.

4. "Spaceflight Part 3: One Giant Leap," narrated by Martin Sheen, PBS Video (1985).

5. Ibid.

6. Peter Bond, *Heroes in Space: From Gagarin to Challenger* (New York: Basil Blackwell, Inc., 1987), p. 231.

## Chapter 2

1. John and Nancy Dewaard, *History of NASA: America's Voyage to the Stars* (Greenwich, Conn.: Brompton Books Corp., 1984), p. 93.

2. David Baker, *The History of Manned Space Flight* (New York: Crown Publishers, 1982), p. 377.

3. Harry Hurt III, *For All Mankind* (New York: Atlantic Monthly Press, 1988), p. 209.

4. Baker, p. 380.

5. Peter Bond, *Heroes in Space: From Gagarin to Challenger* (New York: Basil Blackwell, Inc., 1987), p. 235.

## Chapter 3

1. David Baker, *The History of Manned Space Flight,* (New York: Crown Publishers, 1982), p. 379.

2. Peter Bond, *Heroes in Space: From Gagarin to Challenger,* (New York: Basil Blackwell, Inc., 1987), p. 236.

3. Baker, p. 380.

4. Ibid., p. 381.

5. Ibid.

6. Harry Hurt III, *For All Mankind* (New York: Atlantic Monthly Press, 1988), pp. 212–213.

7. John and Nancy Dewaard, *History of NASA: America's Voyage to the Stars* (Greenwich, Conn.: Brompton Books Corp., 1984), p. 101.

## Chapter 4

1. Peter Bond, *Heroes in Space: From Gagarin to Challenger* (New York: Basil Blackwell, Inc., 1987), p. 238.

2. "Spaceflight Part 3: One Giant Leap," narrated by Martin Sheen, PBS Video (1985).

3. Bond, p. 239.

4. David Baker, *The History of Manned Space Flight* (New York: Crown Publishers, 1982), p. 384.

5. Harry Hurt III, *For All Mankind* (New York: Atlantic Monthly Press, 1988), p. 214.

6. Richard S. Lewis, *The Voyages of Apollo* (New York: The New York Times Book Co., 1974), p. 168.

7. Bond, p. 241.

8. Baker, p. 386.

9. John and Nancy Dewaard, *History of NASA: America's Voyage to the Stars* (Greenwich, Conn.: Brompton Books Corp., 1984), p. 101.

## Chapter 5

1. "Spaceflight Part 3: One Giant Leap," narrated by Martin Sheen, PBS Video (1985).

2. Peter Bond, *Heroes in Space: From Gagarin to Challenger* (New York: Basil Blackwell, Inc., 1987), p. 241.

# GLOSSARY

**carbon dioxide**—A colorless gas produced by the decay of organic substances. Human beings also give off carbon dioxide when they breathe. Too much carbon dioxide in a confined area will cause a person to suffocate.

**command and service module**—The main Apollo spacecraft that carried astronauts to and from the Moon. It was the capsule that carried the crew. It also was equipped with a heatshield for reentry into Earth's atmosphere. The service module contained the engine, fuel cells, and other equipment and supplies that the astronauts needed to sustain life during their trip.

**fuel cell**—A device that uses chemicals, such as hydrogen and oxygen, to create a reaction that gives off energy to power a machine such as a spacecraft.

**heatshield**—The surface that covered the reentry side of early spacecrafts. Parts of the surface were designed to burn away. This carried heat away and prevented heat from building up on the spacecraft.

**jettison**—To drop away or discard.

**lunar module**—The Apollo spacecraft designed to land two astronauts on the Moon. After the astronauts had a Moonwalk, the lunar module would blast off from the Moon's surface to redock with the command module. The command module then returned the astronauts to Earth.

**odor canister**—Canisters containing lithium hydroxide. Carbon dioxide "clings" to lithium hydroxide, so the Apollo spacecrafts circulated air through these canisters to take carbon dioxide out of the air. The odor canisters from the command module did not fit the system in the lunar module. The *Apollo 13* astronauts had to adapt the command module canisters to a specially rigged filtering system, so they could clean out the carbon dioxide from the lunar module.

**Saturn V rocket**—The large rocket used to launch the Apollo astronauts on their voyages to the Moon.

**trajectory**—The given path of a moving object through space.

# FURTHER READING

Baker, David. *The History of Manned Space Flight*. New York: Crown Publishers, 1982.

Bond, Peter. *Heroes in Space: From Gagarin to Challenger*. New York: Basil Blackwell, Inc., 1987.

Hurt, Harry III. *For All Mankind*. New York: Atlantic Monthly Press, 1988.

Lewis, Richard S. *The Voyages of Apollo*. New York: The New York Times Book Company, 1974.

Lovell, Jim and Jeffrey Kluger. *Lost Moon: The Perilous Voyage of Apollo 13*. New York: Houghton Mifflin, 1994.

# INDEX